MESABI AND VERMILION RANGES

SCALE

D1713875

NIGHT TRAIN RED DUST

POEMS OF THE IRON RANGE

BY SHEILA PACKA

WILDWOOD RIVER PRESS
DULUTH, MINNESOTA
2014

Other books by Sheila Packa
    The Mother Tongue
    Echo & Lightning
    Cloud Birds
    Migrations

Night Train Red Dust: Poems of the Iron Range
Copyright ©2014 Sheila Packa
All Rights Reserved
Printed in the United States of America

ISBN: 978-0-9843777-7-0
Library of Congress Control Number: 2014936958

Wildwood River Press
2 Chester Parkway
Duluth, MN 55805-1528
www.wildwoodriver.com

In Gratitude
Thank you to the community of writers and artists in the Northeast Minnesota region, especially Pamela Mittlefehldt and Gary Boelhower. Thank you to Kathy McTavish for music, art, passion, and inspiration. This project was made possible through a fiscal year 2012-2013 McKnight/ACHF/ARAC Individual Artist Fellowship Grant from the Arrowhead Regional Arts Council (www.aracouncil. org) which is funded in part with money from the Minnesota Arts and Cultural Heritage Fund as appropriated by the Minnesota State Legislature with money from the vote of the people of Minnesota on November 4, 2008 and the McKnight Foundation. This book is dedicated to my paternal grandparents Jacob Packa and Helen Konsteri Packa and my maternal grandparents, Nellie Mariana Palo Kamunen and Nikolai Oskar Kamunen.

Cover design by Kathy McTavish and Sheila Packa
Author Photograph by Magic Box Photography, Duluth, MN 55805

"These roads will take you into your own country."
— Muriel Rukeyser

Track I: Night Train

My Geology

I excavate these words from a vein of iron
from stones broken
beneath old growth
from the open pit — lit by dynamite
by men whose lives are punctuated by midnights
who drive new cars to the plant,
to the Crusher and Agglomerator,
and later suffer mesothelioma.
I drive in acid rain
my compass gone awry
over Proterozoic layers with four wheel drive.
These words are test drills and core samples
from the Boundary Waters.
These words are wrung from the whistles
and wheels that turn.
These words have never been projected
into board rooms.
I have yet to wield these powers or capitalize.
I have yet to see the returns.
I claim my words from the broken
English, damaged roots,
Finnish syntax and geomagnetic fields,
from Eminent Domain
and small print, unreadable clauses.
I find my vowels
from labor contracts and mine dumps
factories and invisible contamination.
My words, in the run off
in open streams — oxidize
form like tree rings
in industrial circles
heat in the smelters, pour like lava into steel
form these rails that carry the trains
these trains that carry this freight.

STRANGE HIGHWAY

I was born on the highway
that paved over the feet
of the first peoples
with the weight of gold
over the hopes of prospectors
and diamond drillers
cobbled by the hooves
of oxen and horses
pressed with macadam
bitter with tar and feathers.
I travelled with the magnetic pull
of iron around river
now reservoir now pit
fell on the frozen ground
where horses and carts carried out logs
and carried in steam-shovels
on the Vermilion Trail
that boiled the frost in spring
sunk axles
of the brothers and capitalists
those who gazed
at the ground as they walked
extracted the ore
to develop this continent
made the ships that carried the iron
to the steel mills
built the bridges
filled the cities with skyscrapers
and smoke
fed the assembly lines of cars
and made the munitions
that won the war.
I slept in this traffic
dreamed like immigrants
dreaming of home —
breathed the dust of the mine
heard the whistles and the dump cars

pulling three billion tons
of iron from the ground beneath our feet
heard the sirens that staved the deaths
of wounded workmen
wiped the sweat with a dirty bandanna
waited in the waiting rooms
of Emergency
read the news of the economy.
I saved what I could
followed the Laurentian Divide
joined the union
drank the booze
followed the sun
that rose and set upon the waters
where I swam
lulled by forty languages
and blessed
the hands that did the work
strung the ground wires
directed the lightning down to stone.
I drove the miles of this highway
swerved in cars along its curves
crashed into barriers
buried the mean and sweet.
I claimed my life
from its careless abandon,
lost those acres but not the hole
grown ever larger,
walked upon the overburden,
broken tracks and cracks and erosions
and patches
felt the hum of wheels turning,
the speed that has taken the lives
of those who hesitate or not
like the river with its effluence
like the wind with its residue
from the stacks
like the currents with their tailings
that turn back and forth
settling this earth.

MEDICINE ON THE IRON RANGE
Charles Bray, MD and Mary Bassett Bray, MD

Arrived in the small mining town
of Biwabik in 1899
set up a hospital to treat citizens
fractures resulting from being hit by rock or ore
injuries seen, men caught in machinery
asphyxiation
crush wounds
being run over by a train
falling from ladders
lead and arsenic poisoning
third degree burns on the face and arms
          from lamp explosions and dynamite
miner's consumption
Caisson's Disease otherwise known as the bends
          resulting from work in the tunnels under the lake.
Also noted among the citizens
hookworm
severe infestations of lice
venereal disease
typhoid, diphtheria, smallpox, pneumonia
and gun shots.

WORK

I work as a miner
in the old ways
empty buckets
hauled by pullies on oiled cables,
loads of broken shale
water, compressed
blades of grass,
accordions and old dogs.
In the factory of the past
steam whistles
start and stop the shifts.
Here is a wheel turning
with a sorrowful, mechanical limp.
I nod to foremen and bosses
and beneath, to dirt smeared faces
of men in work boots heavy with clay.
These lives are shaped by notes
in the dark underground
jammed into coal for the furnaces
by the frictions of boom and bust.
We use everything until it's gone.
In these old offices, typewriters race.
The freighters come to port
hungry for the trains.
The engines purr under the ore docks
hatches open for taconite
and the dump cars dump
as the propellers churn
in the turbid water below the surface
where rain can't beat.

North Star

In Hanko, Finland
a young woman boards
the vessel in the Baltic
for a ship across the Atlantic.
The North Star shines in the sky.
She's carrying in her valise
a change of clothes
a packet of seeds
and the sauna dipper.
Distance pours between constellations
between English words on her tongue
through storms and sun.
In New York City, she buys
a one way ticket
boards the train going
across the continent
arrives on an inland sea.
The winter ground underfoot
is familiar with frost
as she transfers to a northbound
along the Vermilion Trail
in Minnesota.
Ahead of her waits a man
a house to be built
and a fire that burns it down.
Ahead, eleven children
to bear, a few she must bury,
the cows in the barn
needing to be milked.
Unbroken ground only hers to till.
Above her, the North Star
inside the aurora borealis, northern
banners waving welcome —

Two Timing

In the old house, a clock.
With each swing of the pendulum, a life span
crossed in less than a minute. A flash of brass
and hidden, a winding key.
I have swung across the floor to music
hand to hand, rough.
Passed a flask, laughed.
Marked the quarter hour, counted night hours
under the moon in an iron bed
slung low to the floor.
Opened the door, closed the glass.
In the crimson heart, a chamber
at arm's reach.
From room to room I fling the dark
myself in it.
Beginning, ending,
too far, not far enough.

VESTIGES

Beneath the ramp, silver
muscled light follows
hidden lines of navigation.
Sky and sea unlatch,
turn back to back.
Without breath or mist,
not a sigh of wind
stirs earthward. Why, you ask?
A pearl is grown by irritation.
Yesterday, it was difficult to row.
Wind filled banners, rifled the water
shifted small stones below.
For a while, knots the sailors tied
to cleats held firm.
After that, lank went taut and
the bolts let go.
Deck hands put out the lamps.
Winds moved beneath the surface
in rhyme, forward and reverse.
Timber splintered to wet matches.
We go unvisited, get through.
A different yesterday
mines were running full blast.
I remember fires blown on the beach,
as seagulls flew
an ore boat sank before rescue.
White pines broke from their roots.
Footings were lost.
Farther, the more silent after —
the sky tolls blue.

MIDWIFE

I am called to the insomniac
timetables of birth
at three a.m. or on the way
to somewhere else.
I drop everything, on my knees,
listen to the body's
wall, watch the private door
that must nearly rupture.
Like a mother, must pace and wait
at the table's edge
to unhinge the gate
and empty herself.
On the other side, waters
break in a ripple
through the parabola.
The naked self comes,
a perilous umbilical journey
on its pale vine
carrying on a correspondence
with death. I smell blood
and sweat in the tunnel
of physical labor.
Sometimes I knead the muscles
coax a new position
help open the bony locks.
Into the palms from the breach
life grasps the air. Cries.
I catch — wipe with a torn cloth
an animal power unleashed, released
that wakes and goes to sleep.
I cut the cord, take
the blue glossy web
of afterbirth to plant in the orchard
bind the wounds
bring blankets to wind the new
into another circle
guide the searching mouth
to the blind nipple.

Not Just Bread

Elizabeth Gurley Flynn, IWW, Iron Range labor strike, 1916

In *Rebel Girl*, she wrote:
"All that summer the strike
dragged out a dogged existence.
We raced up and down the Range
from one end to another
in an old bakery truck, driven
by a couple of young Italian strikers,
who often forgot we were not bread
and bounced us unmercilessly
over the unpaved, rocky road.
The deputies came to know the truck
and took pot shots at us,
so we had to stop using it,
much to our relief. There were
about fourteen towns from one end
to another which we covered.
Several times the strikers marched
the length of the Range, holding meetings
in each town. Sometimes
towns shut off the drinking water
while we were there."

GRACE

photograph by Eric Enstrom in Buhl, Minnesota

Hands clasped, he looks away
from the camera. Out the window,
an oriole sings. He might confess
there were things he misnamed —

he never mended a rift. Years passed
and work never ceased. At the table
waits a loaf of fresh-baked bread
drifted with seed, a sharp knife

and a bowl of soup, just stirred. He put
his spectacles on the book he had always
meant to read. He coughs to clear his throat.
The photographer pressed the shutter
as this moment awaited — arrived and broke
fell into tender crumb, an accident of light.

MINISTRY

Reverend Milma Lappala, Photograph, 1914

A light in the chalice burns,
a marriage of fuel and flame
about to become ash.
Commended to God
all the digressions and processions.
Blessed the lovers who came and left
the husband whose child she brought
through her body, seeds she planted
in the rain.
She pushed back the cold
crumpled the old news, lit a match
in a house of receding voices
doors opening, phone calls
burials and excavations.
Time builds like a wave
and her prayers break into spray.
Her husband will be lost too young.
After he goes, a furnace comes.
In this house of bread and potatoes
she peels the skins and plunges her hands
into dish water. People need to be fed.
She washes the cups,
boils clothes on the stove,
churns her own butter.
In the corners, orange dust covers tools
from another life, ways of the old country
lit by charges of dynamite.
She makes coffee that evaporates.
In this house, she contracts
with the night
wakes to sirens after mine accidents.
Strangers knock at the door
she supports their unions.
She breathes them in and out as vapor
bears every broadcast.
Weddings, baptisms,
midsummer dances.

She saves their photographs
covers the tomatoes threatened by frost.
At day, she sings loud so
those underground can hear.
Her voice carries across water
rides with the rivers that split at the Divide.
Each note she plays from the piano's heart
is hammered into her own valves.

Oliver Mine, WWII

An all female crew
in the pit on day shift —
pickaxe, shovel, crowbar.
They wear work boots

men's bib overalls,
beneath plaid shirts, thermal underwear
and bras stained with iron ore.
They tie their heads with triangle scarves.

They don't mind getting dirty
working in the mine while the men
are off to war.
In the pocket a flask, a pack of cigarettes

a navy handkerchief.
Lunch boxes gray as artillery.
No heels to wobble
after the whistle blows

when they put a nickel in the jukebox
in neon glow, dance to a love song
fingernails stained by toil.
Ton after ton loaded on rails.

They went deeper after the dynamite
with shovels, bent to the task
and took out
that ground they were standing on.

UNKNOWN WOMAN MINER

Cold shop. Bleak light.
She turns to face the lay off.
The company, she's never trusted.
The whistle blew. Inside, hard
to tell day from night.
Safety glasses, standard issue.
Her hair combed from bobby pins
into corkscrew curls.
Fluorescent buzz.
Denim overalls. Kerchief.
Her pants with a hole worn through.
She blows black soot from her nose.
She wears a wool plaid sweater.
Her jacket's slung on the chair.
In the back, a front end loader signals.
Her hand rests on the table. Nobody
doubts the fact she's able. It's rough.
She does what she does.
She will drive home
at morning to girls who look after
themselves. They fight.
It's hard to sleep. Her joints ache
her lunch pail has rusted.
In the back pocket of her pants
she keeps something to protect herself.

Old Music

I was born in the north
beneath boughs of Norway pines that carried
the wind over an ocean
that rocked my grandmother aboard her ship.
She slipped me into the new country,
humming, an egg inside of an egg,
all in her basket and married a lumberjack
in the country of the Wobblies.

I come from the accordion.
I follow the steps at country dances,
come from the sand beaches on the Baltic,
from Kalajoki, from borders that moved,
from the pale white flowers that come like snow,
from Sibelius. One language blooms from another.
The old vowels and new leaves, easily trampled.
In school, my mother was held back.
My father dropped out at age thirteen to drive the school bus.
I was born into the summer fields swaying with timothy.
Into Minnesota. I came after my grandmother's diphtheria
and my aunt's tuberculosis.

I come from dovetailed corners,
from furrows of sandy loam planted with potatoes,
eyes in the dark and roots reaching deep into the soil.
McCarthy was chasing communists
and our poets were blacklisted.
My father couldn't find steady work.
My mother took shifts in the shirt factory.
She gathered pinecones by the bushel
to sell to the Forest Service.

My grandmother remained at the border
unable to cross into the new language.
She pushed us over. The white flags
were the dish towels the girls tied
on their heads when they went into the dairy.

I stayed warm because they burned their firewood.
I lived on trades made with a side of beef.
I tripped levers of the dump rake
behind my father's tractor. I wore hand-me-downs.
My parts were bought from junkyards.
I travelled inside the library.

My mother tied me to her apron,
spoke words that I never understood.
She salted me like fish, churned me into butter.
I follow her threads fraying, broken, woven
into the rag rug under my feet. She was dancing
in that dress. She was opening the bellows
of the accordion when I heard its breath.

I follow the threads back
through her scissor cuts, back through the eye
of her needle. She has wet me with her tongue.
I take her into the American vernacular,
drive her language to its destination,
play the volume on high
in a minor key, old music.

ACCORDIONIST

Violet Turpeinen, 1909-1958

The pendulum of the clock
swung — the bodies in motion.
Think of grandmother's face
when she was young.
The accordions echo time and resistance
inebriate Prohibition
go from straight to syncopation
uneven rhyme. Close your eyes.
The places her toes wore through
dancing shoes gave way
to the rise of smoke in neon haze
a flash of silver light on the mic.
Open the clasp on the case
spread the diamond, lift
the bellows, press the chords
open wide.
The hellos of death, nothing can erase
the bloom of birds in paradise.
No words can place the miles you ride
along the coast at sunset.
You played the halls, emptying your chest.
In the velvet dark, sorrow
holds its breath.
Once you slid into the leather harness
(no voice tomorrow)
hands on the ivories and ebonies
and made the stars race in a steeplechase
heedless.

Patchers

The women arrived through the back door
through the kitchen.
Arranged their skirts,
and for each other, picked up the stack
of worn and torn clothes, neatly folded.
They threaded needles
and pierced each other's marriages.
They unspooled the delicate thread
and cut it with their teeth.
They took up the stack of children's dungarees
to mend the knees.
They ripped out old seams.
They put on patches, darned the heels,
fastened buttons, repaired
fallen hems. In a month,
they would do this at another's house.
They spoke with mouths full of pins,
whispered, chided, decided
the point when there was nothing more
that could be done.
They laughed and never looked twice
at the knots they could tie single-handed.

Broken English

I fasten my syllables
into another landscape,
overlay my words
on roadsides and strawberry fields
and fish swimming underwater
where light falls like a ladder
and air bubbles break on the surface.
My language rises
from the mist in the evenings
from all things spent,
seeds tossed from thorn and pod
fluff blown by what never came
from the iron underground
from trades and unions
from moths whose lives were lost
to the light in the entry
backward through the century
through bellows and steam-driven
vessels on the long tongue of rivers
from smoke and hammers.
My verbs and un-gendered pronouns
gather and I bring to the palate
ragged and unruly vowels.

STRAWBERRY HARVEST

Starting over in the north
after the winter dark and deep snow
old hurts flare.
There are those who do not speak.
Ice hardens and evaporates.
Strawberries ripen.
Her fingers pull each berry
from its green star.
She fills her pot to the brim.
Some fall from the vine
and plant their tiny seeds at her feet.
Some find their way
to other tongues.
The wood violets bloom.
In the night, she hears
the calls of the fox to the vixen
and the vixen's answers —
yes, yes, yes.
Light arrives long after a star burns out.
She bakes a cake, whips cream.
The berries cannot take much handling —
rain-washed is enough —
she takes off their hulls one by one.

Timber

At evening in the forest
I heard a dog yap, then many dogs
then a howl rise and fall
not loud or at the moon
but ghostly
a timber wolf inside a pack of wolves
a howl not of distance but nearness
not of loneliness but hunger
heard the swaying in the crowns of tall pines
a *sh sh sh* that holds the force of death aloft
so hardly a wisp of hair moves
heard not the day's wind
but the wind of many years
arriving, departing
light falling between worlds
into dust and wings
away from motors and wheels into
a strange music for way-finding
a map that changes as you draw it
and a language that translates into shadow.

Fox, No Longer Hidden

In winter, a fox crossed the path I took —
marked the slope with cautious feet
made a hurried leap from dark spruce
into the undergrowth of white lace

into silent snow she floats
through grass kneeling under the weight
upon the clouds of cold.
Her tail is a rudder.

Three months later — it was morning —
when I turned, she was waiting
taking the sunlight into her coat.
She was a red clay halo

burnishing agates with her heat
pouring copper into the puddle
gone before I could reach that place.
Now she follows me

even on this page, I see among the vowels
marked in darker ink
traces of her meandering —
hear under the birdsong

her soft growls.
My lovely hunter.

POUR

I dance on the Divide
run against gravity
and translate the dead.
Tuesday carried me off
and sky came looking with birds.
The world reversed
and the river went the other way.
On the rapids
words flow forward —
words go back.
One deep winter in the north
it rained all day
until the ice broke free.
Maybe the star
that fell into me the red coal
unknowingly sent the waves
away from shore, upside down
to the old forces
that churn the molten sea.
I was iron and under siege.
Tuesday poured me out
in clouds of smoke and steam
cast me into steel beams.

MEMENTO

I found at the edge
of balsam trees, the skull of a fawn
among dry straw and new spears
of grass.
I did not hear the calls or the wolf
(how thin the walls)
did not know this life passed on
so close to my own.
Eye sockets, chambers of air
ivory caverns
a row of teeth hardly worn by mastication—
a fracture and symmetry
taken into my own house.

THE COST

While the maple leaves have flamed
and gone out
the leaves of the small cherry
cling and tremble.

I write myself on these.
I've shed so many things
in my life. I write myself
in the river, in the wind.

Water drips from the eaves
of my tiny house
to the shining blue stones below.
Everything must go —

RENDEZVOUS

I walk between
predator and prey, where stones lay
and blood seeps into places one never sees
where ends meet ends
at a thin boundary barely visible
where new green surges into a sound I can't name.
The city left behind
congested streets blocked and detoured
torn open by jackhammers and backhoes
the past folded like an old map
with weights and measures and sums.
Strawberry blossoms are about to turn
into sweet red fruit. Rabbits meet
where the wild rose reaches the rim of the lake
where means meet means
and waves of the ravenous break against my ankles.
In the thermals
sharp-shinned hawks rise in circles.

KEG PARTY

nothing to lose but our chains   —Joseph Kalar

One night, around a bonfire in a gravel pit
near Biwabik, beer glowed with firelight.
Music blasted through car speakers.
It was getting cold beyond the fire.
A river was falling over stones
through Merritt Lake and Esquagama
clouds poured through the culverts
carrying the moon into Superior.
All my life I listened
to the trains taking this earth away
to the ships in the harbor to the steel mills.
There was a story I'd heard
about the rats in the underground mine.
Some of the workers
tied string to crusts of bread
to drop through the floorboards
in the lunch room.
This was recreation. The rats took the bait
and miners reeled them back.
Now we have open pits, taconite and big plants
with rolling furnaces to make pellets
from the grey dust, a breakthrough
in technology. We emptied the keg
peered into the walls of night and fell deeper.
I brought up the word 'oubliette'
a dungeon with the opening at the top
the word with the same root as oblivion.
No way out.
Some wanted to get on at the mine.
Some were going away if they could.
Some were going to die young.
Below the stars of the Big Dipper
sirens wailed
our voices rose, effervescence
sparks flying.

Rumors

Wildcat Strike, Minntac, 1975

I heard in the blasting
in the pit
the low growl of the cat-skinners
and steam shovels
filling 240 ton dump trucks
carrying the rock to the Crusher

I heard in the machine shops
in the Concentrator
in the Fines
near the bentonite
behind the sliding doors
in the Agglomerator
in the constant roar
of the rolling furnaces
turning the taconite pellets
on the conveyors moving along
the small wheels
amid the vibration of high voltage
through vents and catwalks
the motors surging

I heard in the idling train
at the loading dock
as the dump cars filled
with the steaming loads
in black dust and whistles
from the electricians and millwrights
and the laborers
in the Dry in the lunch room
in the elevator the word
strike.
Whispers —
the weapon of the working man
who gives his life to taconite
a *strike* against the distant capitalists
or corporations who never show

their faces here
and yet draw out the marrow of our bones
quiet preparations
for a battle with an enemy
who fights back with layoffs and lockouts.

Wildcat — unauthorized by the union
— a mutiny.
The next day I turned
back at the picket line
would not cross the men
carrying signs. There were those
that hiked into the mine through the back ways
climbed fences, camped in the dries
to keep the plant running
and not cut off the supplies —
scabs they were called —
skin to be sloughed off.

I listened to the words spat after the end
read the graffiti scratched
into the freight elevator —
exploitation or fair exchange
as a woman listens to a man
an immigrant listens to the natural born citizen
finding between the lines
a noise, a dust, an open pit.

History of the Dandelion

I trace the cross cut of its leaf
to early days
the hollow straw that pulled up the sun's
rays to shine
on families that lived on relief
a grief that once shone like a yellow burst
of star —
the instrument of summer played
to the bare dancing feet —
wilted chains and chins stained with gold.
Once our fathers worked beneath the roots
setting timbers into the shafts
excavating the cold ore
from mineral graves that settle now and fill
with bats
the dandelion seeds float
among the leaves of grass
flattened by our weight.
Do you remember?
Tiny fires of red ants
blankets that drew up the moisture
dandelions' nodding heads
in the shade — endless and broken translations.
Baloney sandwiches
cups of spiked Kool-Aid
accordion music
played in the cow's pasture.

REFUGE

Below the canopy I lay in my bed
overtaken by shadow.
The crowns of the oaks carried the wind
to the pines, and the pines now lean with age
and come down.
Who can bear their weight?
I hear the leaves of aspen
through the open window
wheels spinning on their axles,
tiny insects ascending in bars of light.
The surface of the lake glints like silver-plate
underneath are stones
broken by ice or split by root,
they crack and thud and grind.
In the distance, a strong woman sings.
I pull my knees up and make mountains
I make valleys and deep prairie.

BONFIRE OF ROSES

for Meridel LeSueur

The old roses flicker
with their appetite
turn in the wind, lift
smoke banners from their ashes
rise from the gravel of our reception
indigenous roses
bloom from the cold fires
flow in a river of light
as warrior roses dance
through long years bringing old
ways through the new
drum like grouse in the trees
while immigrant roses
speak in the old tongue
plant seeds and hunt wild game
break the ground
come through the long winter
with new words
look back into the haze
of another history
working class roses wake early
to weld the seams
pour their coffees
into the damp and cold morning
they have mined the ores
made the carriages and tanks
for the soldier roses
that spill their oil in the heat
on the roads they paved
speed through the tunnels
past daisy wheels and sands
as the homeless roses
murmur at houses along the avenues
sleep in broad daylight
on the benches
and in the evening ask
for dollars at the curb

while government roses
nod off to the sound of drones
as petitioners collect signatures
and organs play
as roses offer prayers
and the ones from
the tables donate bread
pour crimson and gold
upon the fields laden with grain
that pours down a chute
into the hold of a ship.
We sway together.
A chain of roses,
broken and unbroken.
Across the bridges
they speed into thorns and stem
and fragrances
as other roses force
the season of healing,
those lovers' roses
that give with their tongues
and hips, open in the rain,
one green fuse ignites
the next as each reaches
into the past and rises
on root and bud and blown petals.

VERMILION TRAIL

I am leaving
the Mesabi Iron Range
on the same trail
that a gold prospector
came in on
with a compass gone awry
and red dust on my boots.
Me, the daughter
of a cat skinner
born on the Divide.
I can say we got by.
In my pocket
is the copper penny
of my childhood
once I reforged it
on the DM&IR
track south of Biwabik.
My father hung
a lead pipe between
two pines in the yard,
the somersault
around the pole
was "skin the cat."
I was good.
I never crossed
a picket line, never
scabbed. Worship
was in the union hall.
In the open pit,
if we got a raise,
that was why.
Payday was playing
a jukebox in the bar,
dancing with a pool stick.
Whiskey was a life
waiting for somebody
to marry it.

I laid myself off
packed my trunk
picked up where
my immigrant past
left off —

Track II: Red Dust

Derailment

The train engine begins
and the freight cars jerk
in the couplings
risk the lives of workers between.
Wheels holding the weight
glide over the lines of sun toward
uncertain futures.
Old rocks speak in grandfathers' tongues
of workers' strife, gun and knife.
Some gandy-dancer riding the rails
between here and the harbor
put a spike in the wrong place —
forgot to throw the switch
by accident or spite.
Companies pushed Indians aside
gave scrip for land
kept the mineral rights
dealt in boardrooms
during the strikes
recruited more immigrants
only to lock them out.
Workers with miner's lung
carried the weight.
The companies armed the Pinkertons.
So many trades —
from Stone to Charlemagne Tower
from the Merritt Brothers
who lost their claim to Carnegie —
the Iron Range spawned the big cities.
The first road
for the gold rush that went bust,
for the iron used up.
Now copper whispers.
In the underground mine
pumps still run
down the long elevator where
men strode into the dark

with carbide lamps
into perpetual damp 52 degrees,
crawled into tunnels with timbers groaning
carried dynamite caps.
Outside, by the tracks
a fence has fallen into the weeds
the sign face down on the ground —
Blasting. Keep Out.
Now is the same as then —
men divided and women spent.
Some words don't translate.
A brakeman empties his bottle
and pits fill with water
the old ones wait for the next disaster.
A whistle blows long and low.
Sun flashes on all the lakes
as the train gains speed.

IRON

A spark was struck
by the iron of this earth
that drives the factories and mines
and lays those tracks that deliver us
to the fronts. Fire roars
in the furnaces, a spark flings
into the dark. We drive it.
Iron's been launched and shot
from bows. Iron has made rifles
then cannons and tanks
has been delivered by planes
in terrible beauty
etched itself into stones
and memory.
Iron has been lit by clouds
from the collision of fronts
travelled on roads
in bones and nerve-endings
burned with lust and fury.
Iron has driven armies
moved with flanks
turned the motors and wheels
scarred the trunks
swallowed the forests
climbed inside the bodies
buried by ash.
Iron bleeds with rust
and comes with its own rules.
Of its tools, I count the hinges
and knobs and latches and pots.
No one has walked upon ground
where iron hasn't been.
Beware, those who sleep nearby
those who have borne scars
the creations and destructions
those with that rage
those with those dreams.

SKETCH

In 1916, in Biwabik during the strike
an accident happened
when the company's guards
visited the house of Philip Masonovich.
Some said it was over a drink
but that's not what others think.
A blind pig was implicated —
a family who took in a boarder.
A grudge unsettled them
a strike at fever pitch.
It began underground where
the intestinal rivers wound
through mineral maps.
It began in extraction of the geomagnetic
fields in the Canadian Shield
with the mining of ores taken for steel
paving the continent
with bridges and tracks. It began
in locations, in mines
where money drained from the pockets
and the hires carried dynamite caps.
It began with fires burning
behind clouds of smoke, the false night
among the silhouettes,
filters turning yellow and wet.
Some coughed in unison and spoke
in foreign tongues, in code.
Some were liars.
Thick ores and clay and blood
mix in crush wounds and miner's lung.
It began in thin pay envelopes.
A bullet found its way out of the gun
but the aim was wrong.
One man was gone.
There were some who broke the rules
and there were stools.
Women couldn't remove the stains —

they buried the remains
but the work went on.
A woman and infant were detained in the local jail.
Wobblies on another road miles away
were arrested for inciting to riot
put on trial.
Some votes were lost — some were won.
A hundred years went by.

BLIND PIG
for Lorine Niedecker

If moon, then only crescents
continuous rough music
of verb and noun
to shine that road upon the lake
trouble the tongue —
keep sonorous secrets.
In the distillery
underground,
work to make ruinous
beauty. In imaging
pare it down, find the essence.
Work double duty
to intoxicate, delete and de-
liberate
expand the seams
increase the proof
stay aloof.
In the condensery
turn up the heat
on the copper tubing
harness the steam.
Pour out both heads and tails
drink wild gleams.

Burial Mounds and Old Mines

In the shimmer of violet rain
along old paths
of a thousand years, along Esquagama —
crows look right and left
into roots that run into old blood
deep in the earth's repository.
Ancestor bundles were taken up
by the tribes
and moved to this site with other bones —
we don't know why.
Glaciers have gone into the sky.
A thousand years of rain
make a high banter with the crowns
of trees while the earth swallows flint,
clay vessels and copper implements.
A thousand years of excavating
and we are paid in pebbles.
Rain comes down like a sigh.
Arrows are pulled from the targets.
Our wars, our burdens are many,
we wait for discovery
in the sound of rain falling on folded leaves
in the silence
before the forest and after the forest is gone.
A fish jumps at the wings of insects.
Birds swoop.

IMMIGRATION

i.

Come into the car
look into the dark with me.
In the knitting
I was cast on or was my yarn
on my grandmother's sticks
in her vein-lined hands
stitch after stitch —
a few of those dropped.
Now a hole runs deep.
I carry the loop
of invisible ores
whispering at night
flights of bats
wind in the tunnels
and farther shores.

ii.

The click-click never ends.
Do you notice while knitting
that progress is unraveling?
Tipsy, motion sick, sleepy
she extends the garment
tries on the vowels
gives them this edge
lifts the smell of hot pine needles
and their roots
as the bank of the river dissolves
takes mud to the sea
murmurs through the night
to bring the long horizon
the sunlight.
She remembers the sound
of waves against the boat
arriving, departing, passing beneath
the glance of custom officers

who stamped a seal on her passport.
Over the border and back
exhaling —
a note sung out, hummed
flung out like a seed in its case
buried and broken and stitched
by the earth who feeds her with rain.
Inside the minerals rise.
The plant grows a root, a tendril
some sort of mercy.

iii.

The hawks kettle
above the crowns of timber
taken down.
I mourn for their height
sing, hold the winged
shadow.
Say all the syllables are
ours — all the lost
lonely, dark
rustlings
breakings, the violence
never meant or done on purpose
short-sighted, mean
steam shoveled
done with an instrument,
all that we buried in silence.
These are new lands
the rooms we built
the dreams that opened.
Of those I am speaking.
To my grand-daughters
and sons, the grandest
beginning, I bless
even the unresolved claims
the stripped and foreclosed —
all things do change.

iv.

My grandmother took in the sunset.
I speak in her crimson —
she always gave with a warm hand
boiled the sap of the trees
for pancakes at the table
at sunrise collected
from the chickens' squawks
a basket of eggs
warm from brooding.
Inside the nests are broken shells
little twigs, feathers given.
She washed the warm eggs
and broke them into the frying pan.
Marigold yolks, some doubled
served with salt and pepper
and a slab of bread
toasted in the skillet
sticky with honey.

v.

I tip the glass.
From the center
from flood and wind
I pour from my grandfather's bottle —
from the accordion
his only luggage —
from the center of fire or star
essential spark of ancestors
that gleams in the eye,
I pour.

vi.

It is late but not for you.
Let's drink to never again.
Refill the cups.
No went on and became yes

what came after is anyone's guess.
Here's to hope
you will bring your warm hand too.
I depend upon it
pour my love and the mothers'
before, give every stitch
of warmth to the cold.
Take heart, the chained heart
the foreign, added-on heart,
the singing of a bird.
Listen to the knitting of the invisible
ores whispering at night,
winged flights, listen
to the wind in the trees
and farther, listen —
love's pouring clear like water.

METAMORPHOSIS

I woke as if on a dark
platform, everything departed.
Raining in the windows
into my sleep
stars or moon or mist,
revolving.
I've travelled far,
the train erases its tracks.
It is not as if I did not know this —
away
is a drifting continent
stone of an iron mountain.
I turn toward it
as if my body were all voices
silenced and listening to the dark.
In the beginning
separation
day from night and water from sky
now me
the way of all things.
The hands are feathers
now
they can not grasp or hold
anything but wind.

BLACK ICE

I go back to the girl
her blades on black ice
crossing visible cracks
fractures fused by zero
on the December lake
over fish in descending currents
silver and precise.
She warms up
the dance
is turn and reverse
intoxication and chance.
She's carving the surface
with hardly a glance
racing from shore
to lift when she leaps —
land without weight —
releasing the pain in her feet
almost blue.
Exertion or fate?
Drowning near
the place she broke through.

ELEMENTS

All winter, as I kindled the fire
my body burned days on end
not sexual but acrid
at the stake
the little girl kept by her father
at the table
to finish her dinner,
my adolescent selves,
the wives I was, a conflagration,
my own immolation of the past.
At the end, I turned into charcoal,
a bear, and burned even brighter
as I carried my ash to the icy road.
All winter back and forth
I spoke with the tongues of flames.
At night I tied myself
to the sound of breathing,
the waves of in- and exhalation,
pulled up my boat on an empty shore.
In mornings when the world
came back, I floated
upon the surface of light,
resurrected and lost my self
to the waters, in vapor
and ice and free.
Noise surged — trees felled
tunnels bored through the iron mountain
my body, bull-dozed.
Ache — another word for gravity
stone crags, granite faces
ledges lifted by glaciers
that came and left, carried by trains
iron strip-mined.
I was weathered and worn
by the rivers that sprung
from underground
with eruptions and slides

floods, quakes, lightning strikes
made into shadow, eclipsed.
I have been travelling
in four directions
borne into the hands
of those doing menial work.
I take this life
to give to the wind, my breath —
with the strings of an instrument
give to the flames, give to the water
give to the earth.

Equinox

I come to the poise
of an empty day —
after winter and before new leaf —
nothing you can see
in the north at equinox
in the trees when sap rises
and wings are passing over
no berries yet, nor needs.
The water climbs
over ice-capped rocks.

In the still frozen mud
frogs, who could have been taken
for dead, jump-start their hearts.

Boundary Waters

Off the road
where maps of lichen and thick moss
take in minerals
beneath the balsam
over the border
past the landing
in the stone face of granite
above the water's mirror
by small islands
where root dives into stone
amid broken limbs of white pine
behind the reflection of day
into dark endings
I reach for my own reaching
hand in the cold water
of October — for a tail flick of a fin
among the sunken shoulders
in a vein of ore.
To take from another body
is a question
answered by loon
or by the morning rime
with weasel
searching the char of a cold fire.
After the urgent
animal of the body —
we rose to a heavy frost
and the moose that trod
over our path
running, hunted.

Conjuring a Bear

Find Labrador Tea
collect lichen
from the granite face of midnight
and pick up the soot of fallen stars.
Sharpen bones
with a rusty file and make claws
out of memory.
Run short of supplies
make do with twine
and pieces of burnt driftwood
whisper a prayer and a curse.
Try rivers.
Willow roots to tie in knots.
Hazelnuts. Dandelion wine made by aunts.
Unfold an old map — find several miles lost.
Add Fool's Gold
hair clippings and nightmares.
Cross the howls of the wolves
with trees falling
in splintering thuds.
Take the wail of a train and its wake.
Old hollows. Hot tar. Lady-slippers.
Neither compass nor level
but blood and breath.
Whatever else.
Wear ice. Chant. Sacrifice.

CROWS

Crows rise in glossy coats
grasp shadows when they land
clasp hands behind their backs
consider the ground where we walk —
it isn't sound, they decide
and fly to another place nearby.
They circulate in the dappled light
gather wind into their bodies and eyes
travel along the highway
shift and jostle one another
inspecting bits of gravel —
if it can be found, crows will find it —
they're appalled at all the broken things
and pleased by rings.
In the rain, they cry with indignation
cannot bring themselves to any unity
cannot become a choir, cannot settle.
They know exactly what they need.

Memory / The Mine

I return but it's all excavation — me
an employee of the organization.
I remember a long road past a gate,
a dead landscape.
Dust. Noise. First the Crusher and then
where I worked, the Agglomerator
with conveyors to the trains.
First stop, the dry.
A sink like a Roman fountain.
Clothes blackened by taconite, yellow and white
hard hats, coveralls, steel toed boots,
safety glasses, the whistle
starting and stopping each shift.
For this, I propped myself on a ledge
for the paycheck.
Steel beams, high voltage. Dripping grease.
One of the crew leaning on a high pressure
water hose, blowing dust out of my nose
into a handkerchief, pushing spillage
down the sloping concrete floors
below rolling furnaces,
swallowing salt tablets from dispensers.
On a swing shift, counting
days till the long weekend
taking smoke breaks, and calculating
what falling asleep on graveyards might cost.
All night and day, the trains came to load
at the ore docks.
In the lunchroom, I took from my lunch pail
a paperback. Kept myself awake
with coffee from my thermos
avoided pellets and their third degree burns
stared into the middle distance
not the ends but the means —
working below the surface.

Stairwell

Iron. Two notes
travelling and landing
on shore and wind-carved edge.
To carry and drop, on rusted

mesh, hunger and freight.
Ingress and egress with railing
between stories — ascents, exits —
threshold, escape.

RUPTURE

Some blame can't be escaped
for the fire.
It happened — didn't it?
Or not just that year.
It was careless. No excuse.
It could have happened to anybody.
It depends on the angle and intensity.
Did I say velocity?
I can't get rid of the smell of smoke.
This changes nothing or everything.
It's too late for never.
The shadow unfolds with its light.
Crowns lit crowns
ahead of me. Behind char and bones.
Ghosts flee.
I went on. It wasn't me
or it was a shadow.
It fills the space that I fall through.

Steam Song

In the sauna, I remember
water pouring from the bucket
to the floor.
The water remembers
vapor and ice.
The walls remember the sap
that rose in the spring.
The wooden ladle
remembers the drawknife and vise
drops of blood spilled along its lines
and calloused hands that carved
the body of the tree.
The hands remember
the hard palms of his father
all those nights working by the fire.
And his father remembers
the draft horse pulling the logs
that remember the height of the white pine
that remembers the earth
before it was fallen.
The stone remembers the blow
that broke it from the mother stone
and bones remember the blood
that spilled
into the roots underground
The nails remember the iron.
The fire remembers the ancient forge
the heat, the heat.

RED STAR

Nothing to say —
they slept and woke and walked
distant theories.
Before sunrise she boiled the coffee
and poured it through a silver
strainer. When they drank
they both looked away.
The star in the shoulder
of Orion
in gravitational collapse
sent a violent stellar wind
too far to feel even a breath.
He looked toward the barn
and she with one hand in her lap
looked at the dog
waiting for a scrap.
On the counter, the tin
of coffee from the Co-op
the Red Star brand
with its hammer and sickle crossed —
one to drive the nails
into the boards planed
from the logs they cut
and one to cut the grain
that swayed in the summer fields
to take to the mill.
Equal shares in hopes
and their demise.
The Northern Electric Association
connected them to the grid.
She made eggs and toast
and wild strawberry jam.
He went out to milk the cows
and she churned butter.
When he came in at dusk
everything was on the table.
He ate and went to the shop to fix

the red Farm-all H tractor.
Pigs had the slop.
The coffee tin rusted
holding old nails
the distant star above the earth
imploding, exploding
hydrogen to helium to iron
burning through the elements —
or giving birth.

HORSES

i.

My grandfather leads Belgians
into the bright sun of the last century.
They clop to the barn door
squinting like immigrants, a smell
of hay and manure and dust
from their chestnut flanks.
The shod hooves strike the blue slate
under foot and give off stars.
They lower their heads
for the door is not their height.
Muscles roll beneath their brown coats.
They cross over the threshold.

ii.

My father grows up in two languages
between his parents' claims.
Leather harness, reins, the silver rings jingle.
The Belgians whinny for a bag of oats.
Their weight shifts.
My grandmother turns from the sight
from the window that catches the sunset
with its fire, in the same house that burns down
on the foundation that will remain
and one lone timber holding up the sky
the same timber the bird chooses for her nest.
My grandmother pulled back
her skirts, kept the children inside.
She's taken her breath away
from his shoulder and throat,
the endless schemes to trade this and that
and now the horses for a gold watch.
She holds her tongue
the air as cold as the potato cellar
as cold as the bottom of the swamp
as the peat beneath the trees

as the St. Louis River that winds
through the homestead and its snow drifts.
Her quilt wears down to fragile threads.

My father plows two fields.
My grandmother hears the Belgians neigh
sees the shadow of an old man
dragged by their shadows. Nights come.

I remember the long traces —
the hame on the collar
that hung on the barn wall
the weathered boards of the cart.
My mother sings the songs her mother sang
and spins the wheel.
The bird weaves the nest with twigs
and bits of yarn,
shells crack open
and two young ones fledge —
to circle and soon, migrate.

Rhubarb

Celebrate bitter things
after long winter
rhubarbs' red green stalks
and partial sun
shared with cutworm and fly
and ants that come —
no house can resist their arrival.
Life's too much or not enough —
savor the undernote of butter.
Smile in dandelions' faces
after the rabbits take other blossoms.
Taste from the plate I've heaped
tart rhubarb
ripe strawberries and sugar.

Neighbor

Far from home
my father stopped our car
and my mother paused in her talking.
On the shoulder of the empty stretch
was a lone woman walking.
The neighbor —
neither parent registered surprise.
No houses nearby, no way to a telephone.
She wiped her eyes.
The edges of her light coat were flapping.
She climbed in the back seat
next to me, bringing in cold drafts.
Her husband told her to get out
she said. He drove on without her.
Not the first time. I watched the ditch.
Nothing more was said. I could see
in the rearview mirror, an afterthought
in my father's glance.
We travelled along in silence,
except for the radio singing.
I listened to the tires' rhythm
on the cracks of the tarmac.
At her driveway, I heard my father's question:
Is this where she wanted to be dropped off?
She pulled the door latch, thanked him.
Later, her husband mentioned the incident
if she wasn't so stubborn — he apologized
while he clenched, unclenched his work hands.
It's all right now, she said. My mother
added, if you ever need anything
just come right over, don't bother calling.

GROUSE

Along a deserted road, at the edge
of October
a grouse between shadow and light arrives
with tentative steps —
as if to say to fox or wolf or husband with a gun:
I've come this far — has it all been a waste?
In his sights the bird
bolts into flight.

Meteor

She burns with a fury
her blood turned to shower
      of star —
in the atmosphere, cast out in high wind
burning in the late hour
night fire — red leaf.
When she returns in the hollow of throat
on each anniversary,
bring ash to the ceremony.
Grief burns in the lung
      in the songs they sung.
In memory, I light her with my tongue.

Consanguinity

for Gladys Koski Holmes

The bear walks over ores
through the ring
of ice and Northern Lights.
A wind from two worlds blows.
I can smell the fire in her sauna stove.
She hands me the switch
birch striplings tied in a bundle.
They've just come to leaf.
She gives me a bear's tooth.
She works at a loom
weaving the steel wire
unwound from a mineral skein.
The meridian moves when she moves.
Swaying in the heat,
I drink cold from the Big Dipper.
She steadies the handle.
One hand, calloused, grips like iron
and the other stirs the atmosphere.
She's made from oils and canvas,
split screens and names that extend
from the landscape.
Inside she is deep crimson and violet.
A rose blooms from a vein of blood
that travels through dark mud underground
and comes up in the sun.
Water boils into steam and the stones speak.
Her incantations come.

WOMEN WELDERS

photograph, Sue Grasso, 1942

Outside the plant, sisters grin,
their hair rolled and pinned.
They wear work clothes
and the lids of their welding shields
are lifted. It's day shift.
Production is up.
The safety goggles gleam
slightly steamed in the sun —
as if they were just called away
from the acetylene torch
and the hot flame of rage
that makes unbreakable seams.
In the plants and shipyards
women just like these
with the air of Amelia Earharts
man the supply lines.
Their feet on the ground in Canton, Ohio
at the Spun Steel Corporation
are solid. Nobody could shove them aside.
Their bodies even dreams are weighted
by heavy aprons and gloves and high boots.
When they go home, they'll sit on the porch
drink a beer, wait for the men.
They dote on babies — keep score
of baseball games broadcast on the radio.
After work, they wash the grime
off their necks and clean their nails
and though it isn't polite,
hawk the dust from their throats.

Martha's Lesson

Dead people's clothes
Aunt Grace brought from the nursing home.
The box flaps lifted as if she carried live souls.
Perfectly good, she said, but with
the whiff of medicine and toilets.
For the children, Grace gestured,
for dress up. But pretend wasn't like that.
It was chaps and holsters and cowboy hats.
Aunt Martha took apart the men's suits
with her seam ripper, to music.
She had been at the sanitarium for TB
pictured in a room full of iron beds
and sessions in the cold fresh air
wrapped in wool blankets
with her dearest friends —
a woman named Ricky
who never married and others
that didn't make it. Ricky sent
another photo later, after they had been
released, posed with a hunting rifle.
She never had a child.
It's just her way, Martha said. I tucked it
inside my head. There were women who
were like men, and there were women like
Martha who hummed and cut
with her shears, added darts, pressed with steam
basted the seams. Sewed the men's wear
on her Singer sewing machine —
she used a tie and a shirt
the same pockets
and buttons and zippers and cuffs
but gave it a skirt.

ZENITH CITY
A Symphony

I haul in with the freighters
glide beneath the aerial bridge
fall into the red grains of sand
walk with the migrating cranes
follow the hawks
rise from the wind
drive the waves into shore
break the breakers along the ledge
explode the light
push back the smoke of chimneys
press against the trains as they come
to the ore docks and back to the mines
then return to the inland sea
follow the creek from its mouth
through the culvert, up the slope
beneath the motors storming
on the freeway, scatter the trash
dishevel the Rose Garden
below the lifting flocks of birds
over young mothers with strollers
stir the dogs by the bookstore
drill with the dentist
cook with the chefs of Burrito Union
on Fourth Street
as the river goes deep
and descending
climb the iron foot-bridge
find the path along the precipice
tip the old cedar
follow the homeless
and student and middle-aged
streets that merge into the city
glimmer in the crowns
of old white pines
find the way under bridges
to the pileated woodpecker
shine in the city lights
over the roofs, to the monastery

and university into the sky
and down again
sway with erotic dancers
and sleep with the dead in the mortuary
come through tar and feathers
and terrible fatalities
wars and old age
read the names on the stones
speak to owls
wander through alleys past kitchen windows
where women break eggs into pans
bring the children home
make the dogs bark
exhale with baby's breath and ferns
in the windows of the florist
shine through diamonds and gold
of the jewelers
through the beds at the shelters
in the paper plants
in the picketers at the clinic
in the liquor stores
fall through the heat of summer
and winter's snow drifts
gleam like candles in restaurants
in neon messages, in casino slots
in shops and banks
and tail-lights of buses
rise in the scent of jasmine tea
and sesame oil and peapods
and sushami
in fresh ground coffee
Italian sausage with fennel seed
and crust of bread and slice of cheese
clatter in silverware
rise through the smokers of fish
and barbecue
through the brewery
spill as foam over the brims
echo through the voices
the heels on the bricks
ferment and pour into

the smudged goblets
come to those in debt
wait in Emergency and Intensive Care
map the body's breath
sweep along the floor
of barbers and barkeeps and bachelors
waiters and Grandmothers for Peace
in chambers and markets and charts
through televisions and sidewalks
and jails
gamble with the lovers
newly met and invest with interest
the patient, the irritated, the separated
come to the first kiss
to silent exchanges and glances
to the crowning head in delivery and cry
to the newborn's father
burn in the tobacco
and fold in the newspapers
come through the vibration
of strings, through the clarinets
and brass, through the hands of musicians
through dark night
through long and sleepless trembling
through pain of needles and rehabilitations
over the bridge and under the bridge
through strokes of artists on blank canvas
through dark matter and despair
cold damp of the deepest mine
and hellish furnaces
through fevers and dreams
come through a seed
rise into stem and leaf
fall back to earth
come through the mist
rain down over the lake
rise from the wind
drive waves into shore
break the breakers along the ledge
explode the light.

THE TREMONT

A stranger checked into a room
in the Tremont Hotel
at the end of the line
tipped the porter a token to lift
her portmanteau.
She arrived — no lady —
in a ruin of red brick with a view.
Bats came in
rodents hurried through chinks
in the walls, vandals
broke the window glass.
The mercury lights arrived
and fell through. Walls
starved down to ribs
and floors dropped beneath
the ceiling's downslide.
Pipes went silent. Spiders watched.
She won't lie. There's been
a lot of traffic coming by.
Trades are not sweet.
Either people are blind
or she is invisible, light
as powder on the empty
bureau where she writes
with the tip of her finger.
Some pray, some get high
chase a train that has long
ago left the station.
With deep concentration
she climbs between sheets of rain.
The hinges of doors creak
and the wind whispers
to the new moon
who will soon knock.

MINE PIT BLESSING
for Liz and Kandace

I'll meet you here
on traces of the deep red ore
beneath our feet
where old growth and mineral rights
have been taken away.
I'll meet you under the sky
on the Iron Range
where immigrants arrived
speaking other languages.
Workers lifted the corner stones into place
from Finland, Albuquerque, the desert,
from east and west
where bears walk and ores whisper.
I'll meet you here among the pines
and thousand lakes
where I swam and drifted as a child
down the St. Louis River
that flowed beneath the bridges
on the Vermilion Trail.
In the magnetic North —
at the edge of the wild where mist rises
and eagles fly
over the Laurentian Divide
where our ancestors
received the rivers' gifts —
to change — turn in a new direction — to flow
away from the oceans we once called home.

LOST DESTINATION

A ship hangs on a thread
above the pews of a church
in Kalajoki
where my great-grandmother wed
where I've made passage
with a satchel
and handful of photographs.
The ship floats on the high notes
of hymns above the heads
and turns on the rising heat
where the pastor breaks bread.
The vessel left port
when she was young
went through the Baltic
into the Atlantic
but never arrived
in Newfoundland.
The names on the head-stones
in the churchyard
pass through my bones.
Oblivious of the foundered
not burdened by dread,
a child laughed
and ran from his mother.
She warned him
in the mother language
beneath the keel
shifting in the notes
played by the organ.
If in my grandfather's lap
my mother sailed, and if I in hers —
what might be found
or run aground
on currents of song
of breath.

LIGHTING

We light this candle
for those not here today
to thank them for the flame
the song and love in their eyes.

We strike this spark
in the depot
for our own arrivals and departures
for those travelling farther
and closer.

The road to love becomes a map
that each of us must draw ourselves.
With the light of many others
we light this candle
send a wish that nobody can extinguish.

.

SCROLL

Birch bark
on my path this morning
after the summer rain along the sea.
A powdery, damp, torn flag
or scroll from the map
of unknown territories
without north, without a key.
From the mushroomed
floor, no mark of seed, root, or leaf.
Whatever was written, erased.
Torsos fallen, empty sleeves.
Outside, bleached as bone
inside, a rosy skin.
I took that scrap and nailed
to the wall
a silence I want to keep.

DICTATE OF WIND

On a threshold
after felling of trees
by tree cutters, dozers, chains,
wind pulled the smoke
from the stacks
and men took off their caps
rubbed their forearms
over their faces and left
as sun and rain soothed
the pitch and stumps
and woke the buried cones
while diesel trucks delivered
the freight of reams
torn open in this room —
each empty sheet
a ground of seeds waking
from sleep.

Even after all the ink
and habitation of myself
as ash I'll arrive
the dictate of wind.

Around the Horn

After the whistle blew
we danced invisible circles
turning the wheel with our palms
around the clock
rolling on wheels beneath our feet.
We blew smoke to the clouds
met the dawn
drank beer from a case
until the sky turned silver
and sun reached the highest notes.
On the backroad
behind the mines we drove
around the horn.
Wind blew upon the mouthpiece
in morning glory
while we tossed the empties
into the ditch
and the day crew thrust
their shovels into the pit.
When we pressed on the gas
the valves of the car
matched the far sounds of the plant.
Train cars loaded
to go to the harbor —
cross arms lowered to hold us back.
The train cars dumped at the ore docks.
Pellets rolled in the hold
below and the ship signalled
to the bridge and the bridge answered
a fanfare for the working man.
Shadows danced
and the plants blew smoke to the clouds
until there was no ground.
Only a hole with the sound.

WORK CITED

Flynn, Elizabeth Gurley. *Rebel Girl: An Autobiography, My First Life (1906-1926)*. International Publishers. 2007. This was the source of "Not Just Bread."

Gunn, Jennifer, PhD. "Compromising Positions." *Minnesota Medicine.* September 2007. Web. Retrieved 12 October 2012. This was the source of "Medicine on the Iron Range."

ACKNOWLEDGMENTS

These poems are about the Iron Range in Minnesota, the Vermilion Trail, and they are stories of travel and derailment about mining, radical politics, unionizing, accordion music and strong women. The book brings together history, geology and a community of people. Thank you to the Arrowhead Regional Arts Council and the McKnight Foundation for their kind support, past and present. Thank you to Minnesota writers Meridel LeSueur, Joseph Kalar, and Sigurd Olson. Thank you to Muriel Rukeyser, Tillie Olsen and many other writers. Along with personal family history, the archives of the Minnesota Historical Society and the Iron Range Resource Center in Chisholm, Minnesota provided a rich repository of photographs and oral histories that have inspired this work.

Sheila Packa, the granddaughter of Finnish immigrants, grew up near Biwabik on the Iron Range. She has three books of poems and has edited an anthology of seventy-five Lake Superior regional writers. She has been a recipient of two Loft McKnight Fellowships, one in poetry and one in prose. She has also received fellowships and funding support for projects from the Arrowhead Regional Arts Council. She served as Duluth's Poet Laureate 2010-2012. More information about the project is available at www.nighttrainreddust.com and www.sheilapacka.com.

The following poems have been published elsewhere: "My Geology," "Strange Highway" in *The Thunderbird Review*, 2014; "North Star," "Vestiges," "Oliver Mine, WWII," and "Medicine on the Iron Range" in *Women's Words* (KUMD, Duluth, Summer 2013); "Vermilion Trail" in *To Sing Along the Way: Minnesota Women Poets from Pre-territorial Times to the Present* (New Rivers Press, 2005); "Steam Song" in *Mesaba Co-op Newsletter*, 2014; "Two Timing" in *The Heart of All That Is: Reflections on Home* (Holy Cow! Press, 2013); "Keg Party" in *Knockout Literary Magazine*, Spring 2014; "Elements" and "Memory / The Mine" in *Migrations* (Wildwood River Press, 2012); "Tremont Hotel" in Radio Pluto gallery installation, Duluth, 2013; "Conjuring Bear" appeared as "Inventing a Bear" in *Prøøf Magazine* (2013); "Crows" in *Write On Radio*, KAXE (2013); "Boundary Waters" in *Cortland Review* (August 2013). Several of these poems have been used in a multimedia and live performance "Night Train | Red Dust" at the Fringe Festival 2013 in Minneapolis. Wildwood River is a confluence of the arts.

CPSIA information can be obtained at www.ICGtesting.com
Printed in the USA
LVOW11s0310050914

402514LV00003B/128/P